DEAF SMITH

Scout, Spy, and Texas Hero

By
Jo Harper

Illustrated by
Virginia Roeder

EAKIN PRESS ★ Austin, Texas

FIRST EDITION

Published in the United States of America
By Eakin Press
A Division of Sunbelt Media, Inc.
P.O. Drawer 90159 ★ Austin, Texas 78709-0159

ISBN 1-57168-063-2

2 3 4 5 6 7 8 9 10

Library of Congress Cataloging-in-Publication Data

Harper, Jo.

Deaf Smith : scout, spy, and Texas hero / by Jo Harper; illustrated by Virginia Roeder. -- 1st ed.

p.cm.

ISBN 1-57168-063-2

1. Smith, Erastus. 1787-1837--Juvenile literature. 2. Pioneers--Texas--Biography--Juvenile literature. 3. Scouts and scouting--Texas--Biography--Juvenile literature. 4. Texas--History--Revolution. 1835-1836--Campaigns--Juvenile literature.

I. Roeder, Virginia, ill. II. Title.

F390.S6442H37 1995

976.4'03'092--dc20

[B]

95-36580
CIP
AC

To Jorge Julian,
another Texas immigrant and hero.
— Jo Harper

For my family, with love.
— V.M.R.

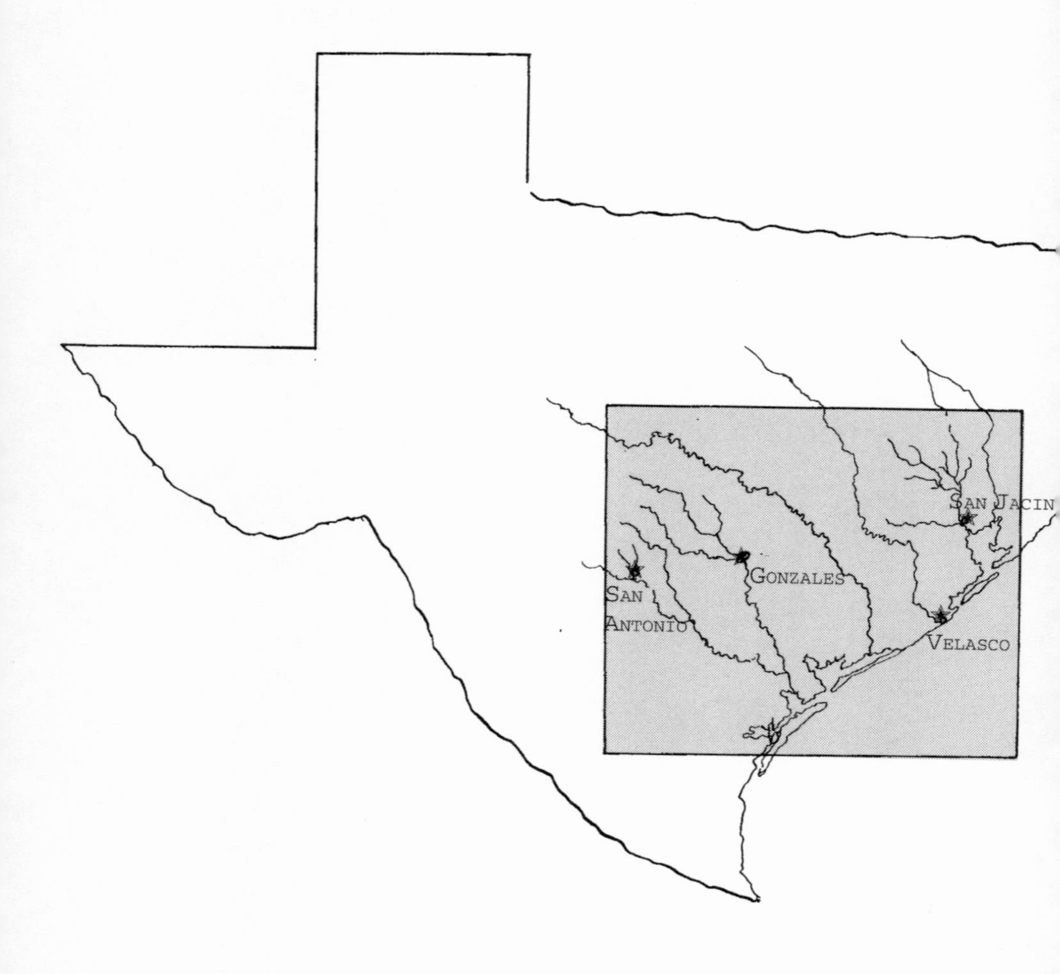
SAN JACIN
GONZALES
SAN
ANTONIO
VELASCO

CONTENTS

Erastus "Deaf" Smith

Oil portrait by Thomas Jefferson Wright. Collection of San Jacinto Museum photo by Hickly-Robertson, Houston.

1. Off to Texas

Deaf Smith couldn't hear for beans. He couldn't hear a coyote howl. He couldn't hear the supper bell ring. He had to look you dead in the face to communicate, and when he talked, his voice was high-pitched and strange.

Not only that, he was a plumb puny figure of a man — so skinny and scraggly, he wasn't fit to fiddle. Leastwise, that's what folks said. But he came to be a great hero in Texas' fight for independence from Mexico.

His real name was Erastus, but all the folks in Texas called him "Deaf" or "El Sordo."

Deaf Smith was so sickly that in 1821, when he was thirty-four years old, he decided to leave his home in Mississippi and move to the wide open spaces of Texas. Deaf's lungs were weak. He had a disease called "consumption." He hoped living in Texas would improve his condition.

He knew that in Texas all the cows had long horns, so before he left Mississippi, he bought a herd of cows that didn't have any horns at all. He took them on a ship to a Texas town called Velasco.

Folks in Texas were used to Longhorn cows. They called Deaf's cows "muleys." Deaf drove those muley cows 200 miles — all the way from Velasco to Mission San Jose. That was a long way for a sick man, but Deaf Smith did it anyway. He had gumption. His muley cows went over big, and that was the start of hornless cows in Texas.

2. Roaming with Rattler

Deaf Smith didn't plan to sit tight and be a Texas cattleman. He wanted to roam. So he got himself a dog named Rattler.

Rattler did Deaf's listening for him. Now nobody could sneak up on Deaf Smith. Before anyone could get close, Rattler would warn Deaf by tugging at his breeches.

Deaf Smith was an open air man. He liked solitude and elbow room. He and Rattler roamed all the woods around San Antonio. They knew the hills, and they

knew the streams. They knew where to find deer and where to find buffalo, where to find turkey, and where to find doves.

They bathed in cold streams and ate wild meat cooked over a campfire. Later Deaf Smith told people that eating skunk meat would cure consumption. At night, he and Rattler rested under the Texas sky while the stars two-stepped across the heavens, twinkling like all get-out.

Life in Texas improved Deaf Smith's health mightily. He grew so strong he could swim a raging river. He could ride like a bolt of lightning. And he could follow a trail where there wasn't a print. Folks from far and wide admired Deaf Smith. He grew famous as a hunter and a tracker.

3.

Settling Down

Deaf Smith fell in love with a tall, beautiful widow from San Antonio. Her name was Guadalupe Ruiz Duran, and she was ten years younger than he was. She had blue eyes and blond hair, and her native language was Spanish. She was a gracious lady.

Deaf and Guadalupe got married. They were happy together. In spite of his weak hearing, Deaf Smith learned to speak Spanish perfectly.

Because he had hitched up with a Mexican citizen, Deaf Smith was allowed to be a Mexican citizen, too. He got a whopping big land grant — 4,000 acres — and he built a big house for his wife.

The scraggly rover settled down and became a solid citizen. Folks in San Antonio admired him. His wife and his four children adored him.

4. A New Town in Texas

In 1825, Deaf helped plan and build the town of Gonzales. Deaf and his friends put it where the Guadalupe and San Marcos rivers meet. It was pretty as a heifer calf — a town to be proud of.

For the next ten years, settlers poured into Texas. The government was

way down in Mexico City. It was a long way off and had a different way of doing things, so there were plenty of problems. A lot of settlers from the United States wanted Texas to stand alone, but some folks stayed loyal to Mexico.

Deaf Smith didn't take sides. He was proud to be Anglo-American, but he thought some folks were roughnecks who just liked to fight. He was a peaceable man. Besides, he didn't want to go against his friends and his wife's people.

5.

Time to Fight

General Martin Perfecto de Cos marched into Texas to drive out the new settlers. Even then, Deaf didn't turn against the government.

But something changed his mind.

In late October of 1835, Deaf and his pal Hendrick Arnold went buffalo hunting on Little River. It was a hundred miles north of San Antonio. When they headed back home, they got the shock of their lives. General Cos and the Mexican army had captured San Antonio. General Stephen F. Austin and his Texian volunteer army lay outside the city. Deaf's family was worse trapped than any critter he'd ever caught.

Hendrick Arnold joined up with the Texian army to fight the Mexicans, but Deaf didn't. Stephen F. Austin wasn't mad at him, though. He let Deaf go through the line of Texian volunteers so he could talk to the Mexicans and get to his family.

Deaf Smith sent a message to Mexican General Cos. Deaf asked if he could go to his home in the captured city. General Cos said he would answer the next day.

The next morning, Deaf sat on his horse waiting. Some Mexican soldiers thundered up and surrounded him. One snatched at Deaf's bridle.

Deaf wheeled his horse. The soldier slashed at him with his sword. He knocked off Deaf's hat and cut his head. Just in time, a passel of Texian guards charged to the rescue. They fired at the Mexicans and drove them back.

Deaf Smith was mad as a cornered rattler. General Cos had double-crossed him. Besides, he was embarrassed to be without a hat.

Deaf went back to General Stephen F. Austin. He said, "General Austin, I told you yesterday that I wouldn't take sides in this war. But, sir, I now tender you my services 'cause the Mexicans acted rascally with me!"

Stephen F. Austin was mighty proud to have Deaf Smith join the Texian volunteers. No one knew the Hill Country as well as Deaf did. No one could track as well. No one could speak Spanish as well. As it turned out, no one was more help to the Texians.

Deaf's family had hard times without him, but they made it out of San Antonio and to safety in Louisiana.

General Austin sent Deaf to serve under General Sam Houston. He didn't know Houston was already headed for San Antonio to help the men who were trapped in an old mission called the Alamo.

6.

To the Alamo

Deaf Smith caught up with Houston at Gonzales, the town he had built. Right away they got news that the Alamo had fallen and all the soldiers in it were dead. Deaf Smith's first job was to find out if the dreadful news was true.

On his way to San Antonio, Deaf met a woman named Susannah Dickenson. She had been at the Alamo. She told Deaf that the Alamo really had fallen. Colonel Travis, Davy Crockett, Jim Bowie, and all their brave soldiers were dead.

The Mexicans hadn't killed Mrs. Dickenson, her baby, or the servants because they weren't soldiers. Santa Anna even offered to send the baby to his family in Mexico City so she would be safe.

Mrs. Dickenson didn't want to let her baby go, so Santa Anna gave her a horse and let her leave with the servants.

Deaf told Houston the terrible truth about the Alamo and that General Santa Anna and his huge Mexican army were marching to Gonzales.

The people of Gonzales panicked. They skedaddled out of town. Houston's volunteers weren't trained and weren't ready to stand and fight. They retreated.

Deaf Smith stayed behind. He had to destroy the beautiful town of Gonzales — the very town he had helped build. If he didn't, it would give the enemy places to hide.

Deaf had gumption. He always did his job, hard or not. He burned Gonzales, the town that he loved.

7. The Scout

The war with Mexico went on. Deaf did a lot of scouting.

Once, near Harrisburg, Deaf Smith and his scouts took three prisoners. One of them was Captain Miguel Bachiller, a special courier from Mexico City. Another was Bachiller's guard, and the third was a Texian soldier that the Mexicans had captured. He was a Texas Mexican. He was plumb tickled to see Deaf Smith.

Captain Bachiller had on a fancy leather suit and a sombrero with trinkets and a beaded band. He was carrying dispatches to Santa Anna from the secretary of war in Mexico City. That was important information for General Sam Houston. With it, Houston could make his battle plans.

Deaf had to get the prisoner and his dispatches safely back to Houston's camp. That could be hard because they were in Mexican territory. But Deaf thought of a clever plan.

When Deaf and his prisoners arrived at camp, the Texian soldiers burst out laughing.

Deaf had disguised himself by putting on Bachiller's fancy clothes, and he was bursting out of them. They were so tight he almost split the seams. The pants stopped six inches above his shoes. He looked like a clown. So did Bachiller. He was wearing Deaf's old, ragged clothes. They hung on him like a sack on a broomstick.

Deaf wasn't trying to be funny. He was being sneaky. From a distance he and his prisoners looked like a Mexican officer with three followers. Deaf knew that way he wouldn't be fired on by the enemy.

Later, Santa Anna said that losing the dispatches Bachiller carried was one of the main reasons he lost the war.

Deaf Smith did some other sneaky tricks too. He even slipped inside the enemy camp. His skin was burned brown, and he pulled his sombrero down low to shield his blue eyes. He would mumble in Spanish and pretend to be a simple-minded peasant. That was a good way to get information.

8.

Deaf's Plan for Victory

Santa Anna's army was one of the best in the world. It had the best guns and trained soldiers, but the Texian army was made up of farmers who brought their own guns. Even though they were out-manned and out-gunned, the Texians were itching to attack.

Sam Houston wouldn't budge, though. He waited and waited. He wanted to make sure the Texians would win.

Deaf Smith was Houston's best scout and spy. He told Houston that the Mexican army was growing. New soldiers with new equipment kept crossing the bridge on William and Allen Vince's land.

“We have to destroy Vince’s Bridge,” Deaf told Houston. He knew that was dangerous — it was slow work and in the heart of enemy territory. But it was the only way the Texians could win.

“I want six men who will follow me through or die trying,” Deaf told Houston.

Six brave men volunteered.

Deaf and his men tried to burn Vince’s Bridge, but there had been rain the day before, and the bridge was too wet. They got two axes and chopped it down.

The Mexicans couldn't bring troops and supplies across the bridge anymore. They couldn't retreat that way either — but neither could the Texians. Now it was do or die.

Deaf Smith galloped back from Vince's Bridge on his lathered mustang. He raced in front of the troops, waving an ax above his head and shouting in his high, strange voice, "I have cut down Vince's Bridge! Fight for your lives and remember the Alamo!"

When they heard Deaf's shout, the Texians attacked the Mexican army. They fired one quick volley. Then they fell on Santa Anna's troops, using their rifles as

clubs and their Bowie knives as daggers. They fought hand to hand. They were too angry to even take time to reload their guns.

The Mexicans tried to escape, but they couldn't because Vince's Bridge was gone.

The Mexicans scattered like buckshot, leaving horses and equipment behind. They looked for places to hunker down. Deaf found a beautiful black stallion. He galloped to a patch of woods where he thought Santa Anna was hiding.

9. A Surprise Prisoner

Santa Anna and General Cos really were in hiding in the patch of woods where Deaf Smith thought they were, but they managed to slip away.

Later, some Texian soldiers took a strange prisoner. He wore the uniform of a common Mexican soldier, but under it the Texians could glimpse a fine shirt with shiny buttons. When they took the

prisoner into camp, captured Mexican soldiers saluted him.

The prisoner was President General Santa Anna, and the beautiful stallion was Santa Anna's favorite mount, "Old Whip" — stolen from Allen Vince.

Deaf Smith took a prisoner too. It was plain to see that he wasn't an ordinary soldier. Deaf Smith asked him if he had seen General Cos. The prisoner said that he hadn't. But the truth was that the prisoner himself *was* General Cos — the very general who had "acted rascally" with Deaf and caused him to join the volunteers in the first place.

Of course, Deaf Smith found out who Cos was, and Deaf was still plenty mad at him. But Deaf was a straight arrow. He was too law-abiding to harm a prisoner, even General Cos. He turned his old enemy in to headquarters.

Winning the Battle of San Jacinto was the turning point of the Texas Revolution. Texas would soon be a free republic thanks to all the brave Texians who fought, and thanks to Deaf Smith — tracker, scout, spy, and hero.

Erastus "Deaf" Smith

Born April 19, 1787, in Duchess County, New York.

Died November 30, 1837, of consumption. There is no permanent grave marker.